365 Days of Creativity

This book belongs to:

_____

_____

_____

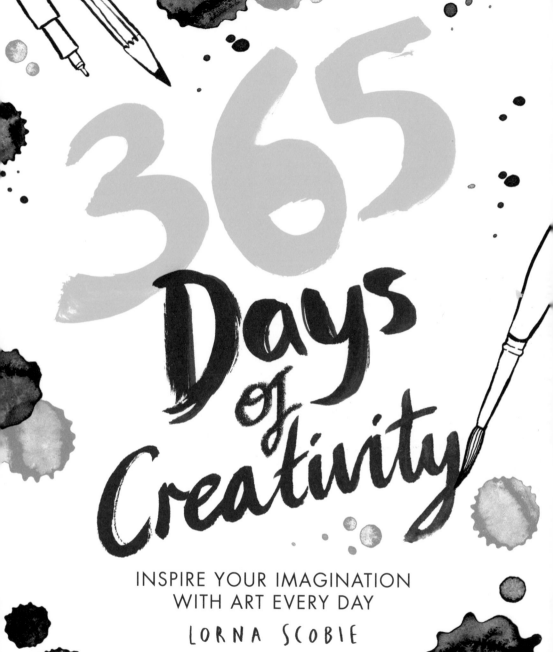

365 Days of Creativity

INSPIRE YOUR IMAGINATION WITH ART EVERY DAY

LORNA SCOBIE

Hardie Grant

BOOKS

Welcome to 365 Days of Creativity!

Perhaps you'd like to be more creative but aren't quite sure where to start, or how to express yourself. Or perhaps you are stuck in a creative rut, and just need a little inspiration to kick start your imagination. The aim of this book is to encourage and inspire a little bit of creativity every day for a whole year, by giving you daily artistic challenges and teaching you how to find inspiration for creativity in your day-to-day life. Although we will use traditional techniques and materials to explore, the activities in these pages are designed to help you realise that pens and paper are only one part of learning how to express yourself creatively. This book is first and foremost about enjoying yourself and creating opportunities to PLAY.

The most important thing to note before we begin – and to keep reminding yourself of throughout this process – *is that there is no right or wrong way to complete the activities in this book.* How you choose to express your creativity is unique to you, so if you feel like adapting the activities – go for it! You may want to use different materials to those suggested, or be inspired to tackle the task in an entirely different way. This is your book, so use it however you like to make it your own.

Work through the book at your own pace. You may complete one task a day, a couple a week, or even just dip in and out when you have a few spare moments. The activities don't even need to be completed in a particular order, just choose one which feels appealing when you flick through. See the blank page as exciting, what could you create here? It could be anything, something small – just a few expressive marks – or a longer, more sustained piece of artwork. Creativity is about feeling free and uninhibited, so rather than focusing too much on technical skill, or pressuring

yourself to produce a final piece, use this book as a space to let your imagination run wild. Allow yourself to make mistakes and discover through trial and error. You may not enjoy all tasks equally but some may spark ideas – if you like something, run with it!

At the beginning of the book, there is a space to set yourself some goals for the year ahead. One of these could be to complete an activity a day, or to use more colour in your artwork. Refer back to these goals every now and again, and tick them off when you have achieved them. You will get the chance at the end of the book to review your goals, and perhaps think of some more creative challenges you'd like to set yourself.

It is often impossible to separate our creative expression from the way we are feeling, and lots of artists use their emotions to drive and inspire them in their work. The activities in the book have been loosely sorted into four categories, each associated with a mood and given a colour so that, if you want to, you can select a task that is best suited to how you feel in that moment. Just choose a task based on whether you'd like to feel *inspired, calm, energetic* or *reflective*.

FEEL INSPIRED These tasks are designed to encourage you to think outside the box. They may act as a springboard for other projects so that you can continue your creative journey outside the pages of this book and develop your ideas even further.

FEEL CALM If you would like a relaxing creative task where you can zone out and take a break, try one of the activities designed to help you feel calm. Perhaps find a peaceful spot, put on some music, and get lost in your creative thoughts.

FEEL ENERGETIC The activities to encourage you to feel energetic are dynamic tasks for when you feel very creative. They may involve collage, mark-making, and perhaps going somewhere new to draw. You might need slightly more time to complete these exercises.

FEEL REFLECTIVE If you'd like to complete a task that encourages you to think more deeply about an idea, choose an activity designed to allow you to feel reflective.

Your creations can be personal and private, but if you'd like to share them, do so with confidence! Use the hashtag **#365DaysofCreativity** to share your art with the online community.

Activities Completed

KEY: ■ Feel inspired   ■ Feel calm   ■ Feel energetic   ■ Feel reflective

1	2	3	4	5	6	7	8	9	10
11	12	13	14	15	16	17	18	19	20
21	22	23	24	25	26	27	28	29	30
31	32	33	34	35	36	37	38	39	40
41	42	43	44	45	46	47	48	49	50
51	52	53	54	55	56	57	58	59	60
61	62	63	64	65	66	67	68	69	70
71	72	73	74	75	76	77	78	79	80
81	82	83	84	85	86	87	88	89	90
91	92	93	94	95	96	97	98	99	100
101	102	103	104	105	106	107	108	109	110
111	112	113	114	115	116	117	118	119	120
121	122	123	124	125	126	127	128	129	130
131	132	133	134	135	136	137	138	139	140
141	142	143	144	145	146	147	148	149	150
151	152	153	154	155	156	157	158	159	160
161	162	163	164	165	166	167	168	169	170
171	172	173	174	175	176	177	178	179	180

181	182	183	184	185	186	187	188	189	190
191	192	193	194	195	196	197	198	199	200
201	202	203	204	205	206	207	208	209	210
211	212	213	214	215	216	217	218	219	220
221	222	223	224	225	226	227	228	229	230
231	232	233	234	235	236	237	238	239	240
241	242	243	244	245	246	247	248	249	250
251	252	253	254	255	256	257	258	259	260
261	262	263	264	265	266	267	268	269	270
271	272	273	274	275	276	277	278	279	280
281	282	283	284	285	286	287	288	289	290
291	292	293	294	295	296	297	298	299	300
301	302	303	304	305	306	307	308	309	310
311	312	313	314	315	316	317	318	319	320
321	322	323	324	325	326	327	328	329	330
331	332	333	334	335	336	337	338	339	340
341	342	343	344	345	346	347	348	349	350
351	352	353	354	355	356	357	358	359	360
361	362	363	364	365					

Materials

You can use any materials you like to complete this book – it's about discovering what works for you. Explore materials you haven't used before, or use the exercises as opportunities to really enjoy the tools you know you love. Remember that the focus of this book is on your enjoyment of the tasks, and not necessarily the end result.

Your materials don't need to be expensive. I have suggested a few of my favourite materials here, but these are by no means a necessity. Visit art shops for a large range of options, and make use of the staff who can offer excellent advice about different pens, pencils and paints to suit your needs. Explore stationery shops which have a great variety of pens and pencils too and browse online for material recommendations. You could also swap tips with friends and discuss thoughts with fellow creatives on social media.

If you are concerned about the materials you use bleeding through the page (as some ink pens and paints might), you could prime the paper with clear gesso before you start your activity. This will form a layer between the paper and the material and will prevent bleeding – just be sure to allow plenty of time for the gesso to dry before you start.

Pencils

Pencils are a good place to start when it comes to getting creative. Pencils range in softness, most commonly from a 9B, which will create a very soft black line, to a 9H, which is hard and creates a very sharp, light line. It might be useful to have a variety of pencils so you can experiment with the different effects they make. Try a 3B for shading and an H or 2H for crisp lines.

Mechanical pencils are also a great tool to have. They still contain a pencil lead, but feel more like a pen to hold, as they are metal or plastic and often have a rubber grip for your fingers. I enjoy using the Staedtler Mars Micro 0.5, and the Pentel P205 0.5. Mechanical pencils don't need sharpening, but you will need to buy extra lead refills for them. Make sure you choose the correct size of lead for your mechanical pencil (it will say on its side.)

If you are using pencils, you'll also need a good eraser and pencil sharpener.

Fineliner pens

It's really useful to have a few black fineliner pens in your kit. These can be used for anything from jotting down notes and ideas, to quick sketches and adding details to artwork. There is a wide range of brands and nib sizes to choose from, so I recommend experimenting with the testers in an art store to see which you prefer. My favourite pens include the Uni Pin Fine Line, the Sakura Pigma Micron and the Derwent Graphik Line Maker, but there are plenty more to choose from.

Brush tip pens

These come in great colours and can be excellent tools to draw with. I enjoy using the Tombow dual brush pens, which are useful for colouring backgrounds, or creating bold shapes and marks.

Coloured pencils

Coloured pencils are a quick, easy and relatively mess-free material. My favourite sets are the Staedtler Ergosoft pencils, which are hard and create a very solid, bright colour, and the Caran d'Ache Supracolor pencils, which have a softer lead and come in a huge range of colours. In art stores you can also buy individual coloured pencils, so you can choose the perfect colour and style. I really enjoy the hues available in the Faber-Castell Polychromos range. Some coloured pencils are water-soluble, so you can blend them with water and a paint brush to create colour blends.

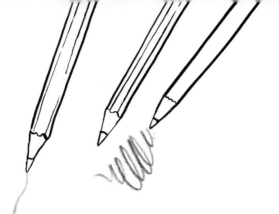

Watercolour paints

Sizes of watercolour palettes can vary. It can be convenient to have more colours in your palette, but the smaller sets are also great and you can mix colours to create a whole rainbow of hues. Daler Rowney and Winsor & Newton both produce wonderfully vibrant colours. When you run out of a particular colour, you can even purchase individual replacements so your set of watercolours can last forever!

Paint brushes vary greatly too, and it's useful to have a range of brush sizes and shapes. Tips can be pointed, rounded and even square-ended, and each will produce a different effect. Experiment with different types. You'll also need a container for your water, which can be anything from a mug to an empty yoghurt pot, and some paper towel for blotting water off your brush. Make sure your brush is wet before you use it to pick up watercolour paint, and rinse it in the water before changing colour to keep colours clean. You could also try water brush pens. These brushes can be filled with water and provide a useful alternative to a pot of water and paint brush when painting with watercolours.

Most palettes come with a space inside the lid to mix colours: a mixing palette. These can be revisited even when the paint has dried out, just by applying a bit of water from your brush. You can also buy additional mixing palettes if you prefer to have more space.

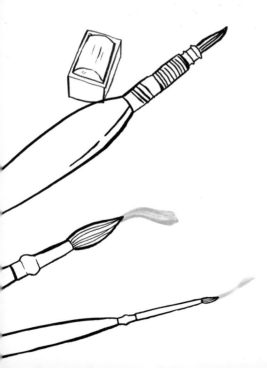

Coloured paper

Coloured paper is something you could use as you go, and you can even use gift wrap or brown paper bags. It's a fantastic material to have in your kit, as it's really useful for covering large surface areas, and for creating collages. It can also be painted or coloured. Origami paper is handy as it is thin, easy to tear and cut, and often comes in a range of exciting colours.

Oil pastels

These are a really fun material to use as they slide easily over paper and you can cover large areas quickly when using them on their sides. There is a great range of colours which can be bought individually or in sets, and you can even buy grips to stop your hands getting too messy! I like the Caran D'Ache Neocolor II Aquarelle pastels which are water-soluble. Just add a little water to your wax pastel drawing using a brush or sponge for an interesting effect.

Here are some other materials you may like to have in your art kit:

— **Sketchbooks:** Use these to continue your creative journey. They are a great place to experiment and record your ideas, and come in a huge range of sizes.

— **Clear gesso:** A primer to apply with a clean brush to paper or board to prevent materials from bleeding.

— **Gouache:** These are water-based paints, similar to watercolour, but provide a more intense colour as they are more opaque. They dry quickly, but are great if you're interested in layering colours.

— **Scissors:** For collages and cutting paper.

— **Glue:** PVA or a gluestick can be used to stick down collages. Water down PVA to make it less gloopy.

— **Masking tape (sticky tape):** Handy for sticking things down quickly, and easy to remove and draw on.

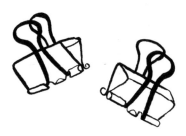

— **Tracing paper:** Stick this over drawings which are a bit messy, using masking tape.

— **Charcoal:** A great material to explore tone. They can get messy.

— **Acrylic paint:** Strong, bright colours, which dry quickly and can also be watered down. Be sure to wash brushes before the paint on them dries.

— **Fixative spray:** Apply on top of completed artwork to prevent smudging.

— **Bulldog clips:** Useful for holding back the rest of your pages whilst you work on an activity.

Goals

Using the space on the opposite page, set yourself a list of goals to aim towards over the next 365 days. These can include anything that requires you to think in a creative way, and they don't even need to involve making a mark on the paper. They could just be about looking at and thinking about the world a little differently. Two goals have been added as an example. It's a good idea not to be too tough on yourself, and instead choose manageable targets that will be achievable.

Consider these questions when writing your goals:

When it comes to being creative, what would you like to do more of?

How would you like to be more creative in your day-to-day routine? Where might you be able to squeeze creativity in?

Are there any projects you've been meaning to explore for a while, but just haven't found the time?

Are there any new skills you'd like to learn?

Perhaps there are some materials you would really like to explore ... what are these?

Once you have completed a goal, tick it off on your list. If you don't manage to achieve your creative challenges by the end of the year, that's fine! There is no rush and there are no deadlines on your creative journey. Work and develop naturally, at your own speed. These goals are just to focus your mind so that you can get the most out of this creative year.

Creative goals

Completed

1 Complete at least two activities in this book per week. ☐

2 Explore a new art material I haven't tried before. ☐

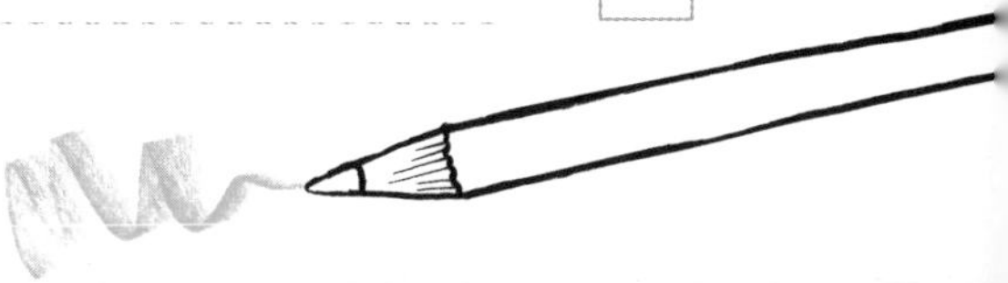

☐

☐

☐

☐

☐

☐

☐

☐

☐

☐

☐

☐

☐

1 ——— Fill the bowls. Perhaps with fruit, pencils, or a random collection?

Explore using a variety of different materials alongside each other. Be playful, and embrace any smudges or accidental marks.

Reflect: Taking time to create without a specific goal is a great way to spark inspiration. Just enjoy the process.

3 ————— Draw the view through a doorway. Perhaps out into a garden or into a room. It could even be the view out of a café door.

4 ——————— Add designs to the snakes.
You could use oil pastels then
scratch scales into the colour.

*Tip: If using oil pastels, tape a layer of tracing paper
on top of your finished drawing to prevent it smudging.*

A colour wheel can be used to see the relationship between colours and helps with choosing palettes. Three of these colours – red, yellow and blue – are primary colours. We can mix these together to make the rest of the colours.

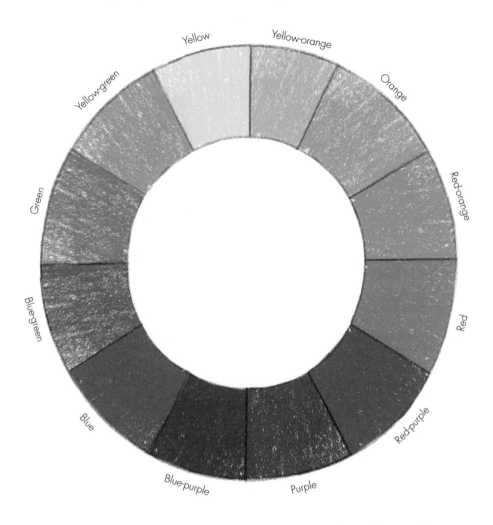

Analogous colours are groups of three or more colours next to each other in the colour wheel. These will form a harmonious palette when used together.

Complementary colours can be found opposite each other in the wheel, and these pairs will create striking contrasts within your work.

Create your own colour wheel by adding in the colours below. You can use any material you like, but it may be easier to mix colours with paints such as watercolour or gouache.

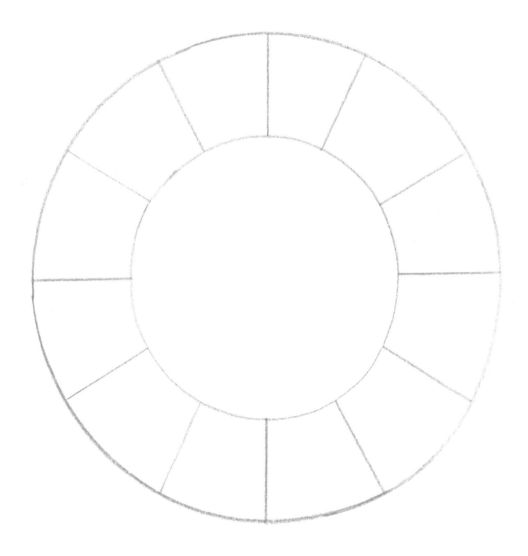

Tip: You may like to refer back to this colour wheel when you are completing other activities. It provides a useful reference when considering your palette choices.

6 ———————— What are the key words you'd like to use to express your year ahead? Write them here.

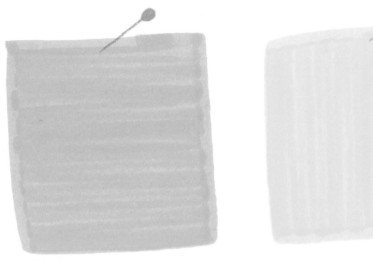

7 ———————— Don't be afraid of the blank space. Go for it! Scribble and make a mess!

8 ———————— What is your favourite colour? Create a swatch of it below. Consider which other colours would look good alongside this colour, and create swatches of these below too.

Tip: A 'swatch' means a little patch of colour, made with any material.

9 ———————— Turn these shapes into something, or perhaps a pattern.

Draw an object on the opposite page using your non-dominant hand (whichever hand you don't usually draw with). Choose your colours first, so that you can completely focus on the drawing once you get started. Don't worry if it's not accurate – you may discover an interesting new style!

Tip: Be patient with yourself, take it slowly and enjoy the drawing.

Turn these blobs into animals. Perhaps rabbits, cats and dogs.

12 —————— Continue the pattern. Explore using a variety of materials. Perhaps oil pastel, pencil and paint.

13 —————— Spend some time today experimenting with oil pastel. Draw an object and enjoy the fact this material is less easy to control than others, like coloured pencils. Embrace mistakes and be energetic with your mark-making.

Tip: Oil pastels can get messy! Cover your finished page with a sheet of tracing paper to avoid smudges.

Collect swatches of materials and patterns that you like, and stick them here. If you aren't able to cut them out, you could photocopy them instead. Write down any notes you have about the pattern.

Fun design — could be a good colour palette too.

15 ———————— Whilst you are watching TV, draw the faces of the people that you see.

Tip: You may only have a few seconds to capture each person, so try to remember their key features. Don't be too precious, move on to the next drawing as soon as you are inspired to draw somebody else.

16 ———— Design a wallpaper for this wall, and draw some pictures in the frames.

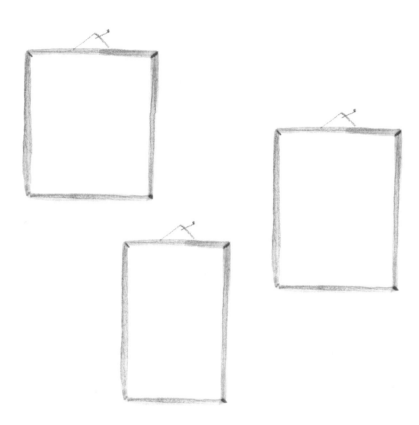

17 ———— Continue the pattern. Don't worry if it's not perfect, just enjoy the act of being creative and using colour.

Windows make great natural frames for your artwork. Draw what you might see through a train window.

19 —————— Explore using different materials. Let your mind switch off as you just enjoy the process of selecting colours and materials to use. Try oil pastels, coloured pencils, watercolour, pens and coloured paper.

20 —————— Look up. Draw something that you can see above you. Perhaps a light shade, a tree or view from a window. Try and draw from a perspective that you wouldn't usually draw.

21 ———— Draw lots of little things from your day. You could do this as you go, or at the end of the day from memory.

Explore using cut-out paper shapes in a collage. Rather than discarding the paper you've cut the shape from, use these 'negative space' pieces in your collage too, and any extra materials you feel like. Try activity 83 to decorate a vase using the technique you have experimented with here.

Tip: When using a glue stick on tissue paper, apply it slowly to avoid tears.

23 ———— Design some pairs of socks.

24 ———— What is in the jars? Food? Butterflies? Something unexpected?

25 ——————— Using only this palette of colours, create an underwater scene. You could use cut paper, or any other material you like. Perhaps the scene is abstract, or maybe it looks realistic?

Tip: You may need to mix paint to achieve the exact colour in the palette. You can also paint coloured paper before cutting it, so that it's the colour you are after.

Create a jungle. What might you fill it with? Allow the trees and plants to overlap and intertwine to emphasise the wildness.

27

You are never out of ideas, it's just that some ideas are more appealing than others. Use the space below to write down as many ideas for creative projects as you can. No matter how small or large, each idea is valid and there is no right or wrong.

Perhaps an idea you are excited by will leap forwards. When you have finished, look through your ideas and circle the ideas you would like to progress now, or at a later date.

Reflect: It's useful to do this activity every couple of months, so you will get a chance to revisit it later in the book.

——————— Add patterns to these geometric shapes.

29 ———— Turn these coloured blobs into cacti and succulents. Add details like exotic flowers, pots, insects and birds. Perhaps the plants are in a rock garden, and you draw the surrounding pebbles and other plants.

30

New views and environments can spark new ideas. How many different places could you visit and explore in your local area? Parkland? A river? A forest? A town?

List or sketch them here.

Reflect: Perhaps take a sketchbook to these places and record anything that inspires you. This could be an interesting object or view, or a set of colours you enjoy.

31 ———— Artwork with blue and green hues can create a very calm mood. Explore this below, by using only blue and green materials. Try to channel serenity as you go.

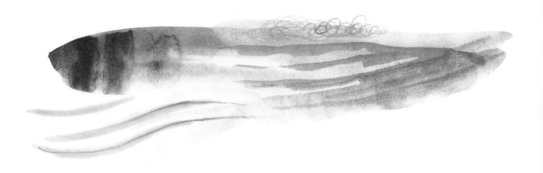

Create concentric shapes in the squares below.

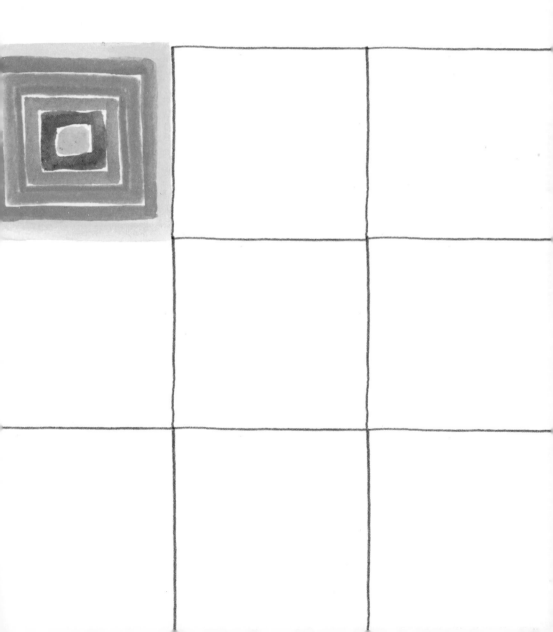

Explore using two different materials together, like oil pastels and watercolour paints. Have a play and see what marks and textures you can create.

Reflect: Perhaps exploring these materials will inspire a new way of creating art. Jot down any ideas you have for future pieces of art.

—————— Create a scene around the runners to show where they are running.

35 —————— Draw a spring landscape around the trees. Perhaps add leaves to the trees and animals living under them, or in their branches.

36 —————— Create a pattern using two complementary colours. Refer back to your colour wheel in activity 5.

Create a collage of things that inspire you. This could be patterns, colour swatches or even different materials.

Reflect: What made you choose these things? Why do you like them? Once you have identified this, you might like to start considering these elements and ideas when you are working on your own creative projects.

38 ———— Draw somebody moving. Maybe someone walking past a café, or someone in your home doing household chores, such as carrying washing. How are they leaning? Where is the weight in their bodies? Show the weight and angles of their bodies in the lines you make. Explore how the thickness of your line shows the movement and weight. Be confident in your mark-making.

Look for creative inspiration wherever you go. Look around you when you are out having dinner or sitting in a café. What are the shapes, objects or colours which interest you?

Draw them here. They could be as unusual or everyday as you like.

Tip: Perhaps carry a small sketchbook and a couple of coloured pencils when you are out and about, so that you can record things that inspire you. If you can't draw things while you are still looking at them, draw them as soon after as you can.

Sometimes the idea of drawing a whole figure or scene can feel very daunting. We can overcome that feeling by focusing first on the smaller elements of the scene, or figure, that are most difficult to draw, such as the hands. Decide on what you'd like to draw – perhaps a person or scene in your house – and spend up to an hour practising drawing the most difficult elements.

If you enjoy these studies, there will be an opportunity to expand on what you have done here in activity 273.

Tip: Draw with whatever material feels natural. This activity is all about exploring and experimenting, so perhaps try a variety of materials.

Reflect: What have you learnt from these studies? Perhaps you've found a particular way of representing the shadow, or a good colour for the lines.

41 ———— Think of one of your best friends or a close family member. Create a pattern that reminds you of them, thinking about the colours and shapes that best represent what they mean to you.

42 ———— Fill the shelf with objects. Perhaps some paintings, books, plants and art materials.

Continue the design, adding your own ideas. Perhaps use cut paper as your base.

44 ———— Add designs to these teapots. You could use cut tissue paper to add blocks of colour.

Tip: Place tissue paper on top of the teapot, then trace the shape onto it. You then have a guide of where to cut your shapes.

45 ———— Continue the pattern. Use a brush with a square tip if you have one, or any other material you like.

46 ——————— If you are feeling like you would like to draw or be creative, but are slightly stuck for inspiration, try mixing up your environment. If you usually use this book, or your own sketchbook, in one place, go somewhere different to think. You could go for a walk, have a look around a garden or even just change room. Take some time to let your mind wander in this new place. What ideas come into your head? Perhaps an idea for a new piece of art, or a pattern? Use the space below to explore.

Tip: It's useful to do this without any distractions, so choose a quiet spot, or walk without music. Give your mind the freedom to think.

47 ———————— Create little thumbnail pictures using cut paper. This is a great opportunity to use bold colours and graphic shapes.

48 ——————— Draw a sea. You could start with watercolour paint, and allow the colours to blend into each other. Or perhaps use oil pastels, which can then be blended together using your finger. Suggest movement by making energetic marks, or by using torn pieces of coloured paper.

Create colourful bunting.

Seek out interesting characters who inspire you to draw. Perhaps you see someone when you are out who is very striking. Look carefully at them, then draw what you remember seeing when you get the chance. What are they wearing? What do they say?

How DARE that individual?

Tip: You may want to note down key things about their appearance straight away, or perhaps something they've said.

51

Encourage yourself to think creatively by drawing a scene with a limited colour palette. Choose 6–10 colours, and try to avoid black. Draw something you can see, keeping your lines loose. If you don't have the correct colour in your palette, work with what you've got and choose the next closest colour.

Tip: Enjoy the process and relax! You could even deliberately use completely different colours to what you see in front of you. Don't worry about making a mistake.

Add plants to the pots.

53 ———————— Draw a self-portrait using any material you like. Find a mirror and draw what you see. Perhaps use cut paper to create larger shapes of colour.

54 —————— Sometimes, being creative is as simple as taking the time to observe the world around you. Today, try to find the entire alphabet from A–Z when you are out and about. You might see letters in street signs, or in logos on clothing. Note down when you find each letter.

55 —————— Design an imaginary animal.

Fill the table. Perhaps there are plates of food, fresh fruit, flowers in a vase or piles of books. Try not to worry about the perspective being right, just enjoy taking the time to be creative.

57

Hold two coloured pencils together, and draw with them both at the same time. Perhaps create a pattern, doodle or even an observational drawing.

Draw the flamingos in the water.

Reflect: Some of the bodies may overlap.
How will you approach this?

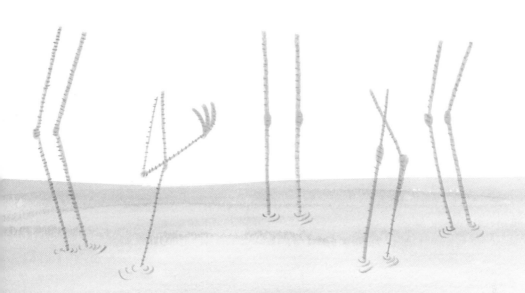

Visit somewhere where there are people being active, such as a park, beach or town. Draw the people you see moving around.

Are they interacting with each other? Keep your lines fast and energetic, to help communicate the sense of movement.

Complete the other halves of these leaves.

Taking time to explore the different effects you can create with your materials is very important. Feel confident with your tools, and have fun making marks with them. Use the space below to make marks and lines with your different colours and materials.

Continue the pattern using coloured paper squares. Add patterns or graphic designs to the boxes.

Using only these geometric shapes, draw an object.

65 ———————— One way to overcome any fear of the blank space you might have is to just go for it. Draw a line. Now another. And another. Relax, and see where the lines take you.

Using your imagination, design a cereal packet. You could show a bowl of the cereal in the background.

67 ———— Draw your hands.

68 ———— Design the plates.

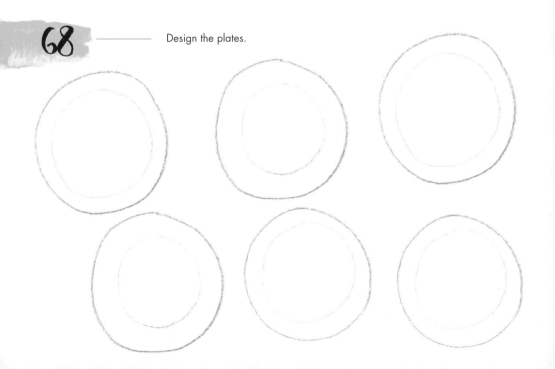

Use lots of different materials to add colour to the rainbow.

70

Encourage yourself to work *with* your mistakes, rather than correcting them. Use a pen, or another material that can't be erased. Draw a page full of people. Keep drawing, keep exploring and if you make mistakes, try to correct them, or move on to the next drawing.

Tip: You could draw people in your house, in a café, or even from the television.

—————— Colour in the stripes.

72 ———— Create a pattern using only straight lines and angles.

73 ———— Write down everything you are thinking below without pausing. Allow your mind to wander freely. Writing down our thoughts and ideas can help us be more creative generally, and unclog any creative blocks.

74

Create a field of flowers by adding detail to these colourful blobs. Add details and stalks, and perhaps insects, leaves and grass.

Draw things that are circles. Food, planets, toys?

76 —————— Draw a collection. It could be a collection of anything that interests you. If you don't feel like drawing, you could cut images from a catalogue or magazine and create a collage.

77 ——————— Go on an inspiration hunt. Flick through a book, or a whole shelf of books. Use the space below to note down or doodle creative ideas that come to mind.

78 ——————— Explore creating colour palettes using analogous colours. Refer back to your colour wheel in activity 5.

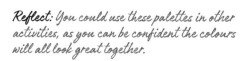

Tip: A colour palette is a group of colours that you may choose to use together. Create a blob, or 'swatch' of each colour, as has been done here with this green and yellow palette.

Reflect: You could use these palettes in other activities, as you can be confident the colours will all look great together.

79 ———— Fill the flats with life.

Mono-printing is a form of print-making where you create one unique piece of art – hence 'mono-printing'. Follow the steps below to try it for yourself with oil pastels, using the space on the opposite page to experiment.
You will have an opportunity to create a still life and a pattern using this technique later on in the book.

1. Start by finding a clean sheet of thin paper. Use oil pastels to cover an area on the sheet of paper with colour.

2. Lay this, coloured side down, on another piece of paper or the opposite page.

3. Carefully draw with a sharp pencil on the reverse side of the coloured paper. The oil pastel will transfer to the new piece of paper wherever you have drawn on it.

Tip: Use a hard, sharp pencil or mechanical pencil to make your marks.

4. Whilst holding the coloured paper down firmly, lift up a corner to check your colours are aligned and you are drawing in roughly the right place.

5. Try straight lines and block shapes.

6. Experiment with layering colours. Draw on top of one colour first, then move the paper around so a new colour is lined up with your drawing.

Line up some objects in front of you. Do a continuous line 'blind' drawing of them – so look only at the objects as you draw, not the page, and don't lift your pen from the page. Work from one side to the other.

Tip: Enjoy the process of looking and drawing. Don't worry about accuracy, this activity is meant to be fun and peaceful!

82 —————— Draw today's sky and weather. Work quickly and express the mood using colour and mark-making. If it is windy, perhaps physically draw the direction of the wind.

83 ——————— Using the process you explored in activity 22, decorate this vase using cut-out paper. Don't forget to use the negative shapes that are left over after you have cut something out.

Tip: Perhaps add flowers into the vase, and use the negative shapes from the leftover paper on the vase itself.

84 ———— Set a timer, and draw as many animals as you can in 10 minutes. Don't worry about your drawings being 'good' or 'bad' – this activity should help you loosen up and feel inspired.

85 ———— Fill this area with drawings of waves.

86 ——————— Fill each block with a different pattern.

87 ——————— Create a collage of a landscape scene using paper torn out of newspapers and magazines.

88 ——————— Go out of your comfort zone. Read a book of a genre that you wouldn't usually pick up, or watch a film you'd never usually choose. Does it challenge the way you think? Write down any ideas you get from trying something new.

89 ——————— What kind of creative people inspire you? What traits do they have that you could incorporate into your life?

90 ———— Create a map of somewhere important to you. This could be somewhere imaginary, or from memory, and it doesn't need to be accurate.

91

Fill the page with circles using oil pastels. Enjoy the rough texture they make, and explore how using different angles and pressures alters the look of your circles.

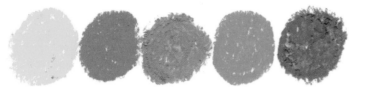

Look out for creative inspiration throughout your day. Perhaps when you are making breakfast you see shapes or colours which inspire you to draw. Your subject matter could be the most everyday object – like these eggs. Explore drawing an everyday object or food on the opposite page.

Design three masks. What could they be used for?

Design the tiles.

95

Using cut paper, create a striking scene or abstract design on this black background.

—————— Draw the weather today.

97 ———— Draw people interacting with each other. Add the features of the face, starting with eyes about halfway down the head. What are they saying or doing?

98 ———— Make yourself a cup of tea or coffee. Now, try and draw it before it gets cold.

Inspiration can come from anywhere. Sit at a window and look outside, perhaps at home or in a café. Draw six things you haven't noticed before.

*Tip: Before you begin, spend a couple minutes just looking.
Perhaps you notice some wildlife, a group of colours you like,
or even a sound. How would you capture this on the page?*

100

Using only the colours in the palette below, create a pattern. You don't have to use all the colours, and you could use some colours a lot more than others.

Tip: Perhaps choose one of the bolder colours to be your 'accent' colour. This is when a colour is used sparingly to enhance the rest of the colours in a design.

Making the first
mark on the page is
the hardest part,
so take a breath,
be bold and make
yours now.

Continue to add to the design using torn paper.

Reflect: You could use this technique to create some horizons, using torn paper to represent the sky, sun and land.

Create designs for the flags.

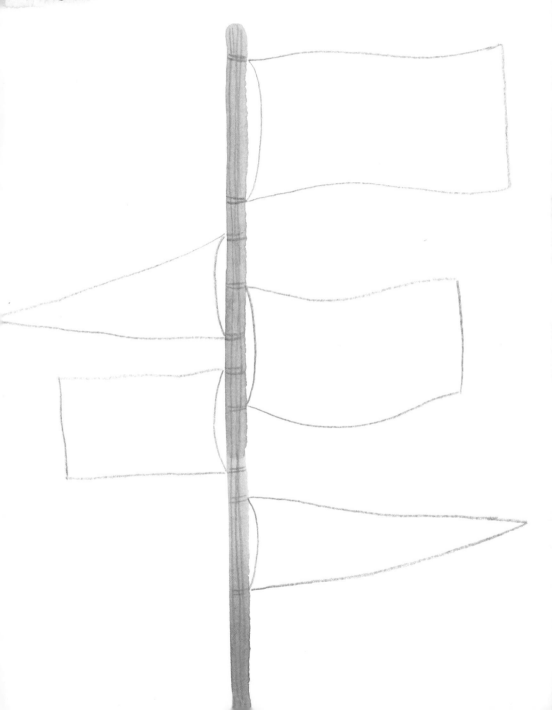

Create some hand-lettering for the word CREATIVE.

104

Fill the page with big gestural brush marks. Perhaps this could become a larger piece of art?

105

Find a photograph of a person. Turn it upside-down and draw it here. Drawing upside-down helps us to see a familiar subject as shapes and lines, so we draw what we see, as opposed to what we expect to see. This may mean you create a more accurate drawing.

Reflect: Turn the book around once you've completed your drawing. How does it look?

Create a pinboard of inspiration. Collect postcards, clippings and ideas that inspire you. Attach them here, or even create a real pinboard at home.

Continue the pattern.

108 ——————— Design a sign for your home. Perhaps a door number, or a beautifully handwritten name. Could this be something you create for real?

109 ——————— Draw three things that you love.

Visit somewhere like a café, restaurant or bar and sketch some of the smaller details that you see.

Ingredients

Bar snacks

Light fitting

Reflect: Taking your sketchbook somewhere new can be a great way to inspire ideas, because you will be looking at a whole new set of things.

111 ——————— What is along the river bank?

112 ——————— What are your hobbies? How could you combine these interests with creativity? If you enjoy reading, could you draw the characters from your favourite book, or create your own? Write down some ideas here.

Create patterns in the white stripes. You could limit yourself to just a few colours – or perhaps just black and white.

Fill the page with doodles. Let your mind wander.

115

Draw the sky above some buildings, trees or whatever landscape you can see. Focus on the colours in the clouds and sky, rather than the objects in the foreground, which you may choose to draw simply as silhouettes. Use whichever materials you feel inspired by.

Reflect: Are any parts of the clouds truly white?

Tip: You may have to work quickly if the clouds are moving fast. Begin by sketching the shape of the clouds, then use paint, or the side of a coloured pencil to cover large areas quickly. It's great if your clouds look rough – it can add to the energy of your drawing.

Practise controlling your brush by continuing the pattern up the page. Use a square-tipped brush if you have one, and take it slowly.

117 ——————— Be collaborative. Meet with friends or family and spend some time discussing creative ideas, or drawing together. Perhaps you could discuss craft ideas for your home, or ideas for pieces of art.

Draw some people using the incorrect colours. Rather than drawing the colours you see, draw with wild purples, blues and oranges.

119

—————

We all experience creative bursts at different parts of the day. Find out when you are most creative. Choose an object as a subject and draw it at four different times of the day, from first thing in the morning to late evening.

Tip: Choose whatever material feels right in the moment – it can be different each time.

Time:

Time:

Time:

Time:

Reflect: At what time of day do you feel most inspired? When did the activity feel the most natural?

120

Draw the outfit you are wearing today. Label the items of clothing with any particular details about them, or memories you have of where you bought them.

121

Fill the page with blobs of colour, using coloured pencils. Try blending colours together on top of each other to see the effects.

122 —————— What are you thankful for? Draw or write your answers below.

123 —————— The sea can be so many different shades of blue, green and grey. Create swatches below exploring this, considering all the colours you might see in the water.

Add colour and pattern to the floral design. Consider your colour palette before starting, and the mood you'd like to convey. Fresh? Autumnal?

Continue adding to the image and make it your own. Are they really flowers, or just the print on someone's dress?

Look at a photograph you love. Below, create swatches of all the colours you can see. Draw or paint parts of the photograph that you love.

Continue the design by adding straight lines in coloured pencil.

In five words, describe the smell of spring. Now draw it.

Combine two different materials and create swatches below. Perhaps creating these will spark ideas for further projects, add notes to your swatches where they do.

oil pastel & watercolour	watercolour & oil pastel	tissue paper & watercolour	watercolour & coloured pencil
oil pastel & tissue paper	brush pen & fineliner pen		

Reflect: You may like to refer back to this page for inspiration, when choosing materials for a future activity.

130

Consider all the different styles of art, from abstract to very realistic. Choose an object and draw it four times; each time using a different style that you'd like to explore.

Style:

Style:

Style:

Style:

131

A great way to encourage yourself to think creatively is to focus on the things that inspire you. Fill this page with drawings of items, ideas, or even places that you love.

132 ———— Continue the coloured lines. Practise controlling the material and keep as close to the previous line as you can, without touching it.

133 ———— Draw your favourite animal or animals.

134 ——— Ask a friend or family member what they enjoy most about your creative journey so far.

135 ——— Draw a winter landscape around the trees. You could add foliage and animals to the trees. Perhaps add people too, bracing against the cold.

136 ——————— Design some wrapping paper. Perhaps you could create your own wrapping paper by customising rolls of blank paper?

Fill the frames with artwork. These could be based on other pieces of artwork you admire, or be entirely new creations.

Colour in the triangles to create a pattern.

139 ——————— Visit your local foodhall or market. Draw what interests you. Is it the people you see? The food? Packaging and colours?

140 ————— Fill each block with colours and shapes that you associate with particular moods. How would you represent happy? Or peaceful?

141 ———— List the things in your life that get in the way of daily creativity. How could you adjust some of these to make it easier for you to create?

142 ———— Using only these geometric shapes, draw a face.

Add colour and designs to the seahorses. Perhaps paint the sea around them.

144

Explore applying different pressures as you move your paintbrush, pen, pencil or pastel across the page.

Brush pen

Oil pastel

Watercolour (thick brush)

Using the skills you learned in activity 80, create a drawing of an object or scene using the mono-print technique.

Tip: As you will be using oil pastels, this can get a bit messy. Once you've completed your drawing, you may like to protect your page from smudging by attaching a layer of tracing paper, or by spraying with a fixative. Embrace the accidental marks and imperfections as you go.

Reflect: This is a great way to switch off from the worries of daily life as it does take a bit of concentration. You might find yourself getting completely lost in the task.

Add flowers and designs to the vases.

147 —————— There are so many different shades of green. Create swatches of lots of different greens here, using different materials.

Tip: You may want to create your own shades, by mixing together different blues and yellows.

148 —————— Fill this space with the name of someone you love. Use different mediums such as pencil, oil pastels or watercolour.

149 ————— Try colour blending with watercolour, allowing the different colours to bleed into each other.

Reflect: Could these splodges become anything else? An object?

150 ————— Add life to the forest.

151

Use the colour swatches below to inspire a drawing or painting of an outdoor scene. Perhaps an imaginary location, or somewhere from memory. What do the colours make you think of?

Design gift wrap for these presents.

153

Choose two complementary colours from the colour wheel you made in activity 5. Draw a face using just these two colours. You can use any material you feel comfortable with.

Reflect: How does using complementary colours affect the feel of the drawing?

Turn these blobs of colour into flowers.

155

It can be really rewarding to spend time with friends, being creative. Invite a friend round to draw with you. Set up a scene, or choose a subject for you both to draw – perhaps even each other.

Reflect: How have you and your friend tackled the drawing in different ways? What do you like about their drawing? Perhaps they have used a different technique to you, or can share some tips and ideas?

156

Fill the page with drawings of profiles of faces. This is the view of the side of the face. Rather than drawing the face itself, just draw the negative space around the face.

Tip: Look carefully at the faces you are drawing and the angles and shapes you see around them. This exercise helps us to understand complex shapes, such as faces, and simplify them to make them easier to draw.

Draw under the ground. Perhaps there are tunnels or hidden burrows?

Turn these shapes into trees or a forest.

159 ———— Go on an inspiration hunt: visit a gallery and look at the artwork. Note down any ideas or thoughts that spring to mind. This might be about composition, subject matter, colour or ways of working.

Tip: If you are unable to visit a gallery or museum, visit the web page of a gallery instead and browse the images.

160 ———— Design a pair of trainers (sneakers).

161

Just using torn and cut paper to collage, create a landscape scene. Perhaps add hints of human life, or keep it completely wild.

Draw some houses that are in your street, or nearby.

Tip: Perhaps use watercolour paint to create washes of colour, or draw in line.

163 ———————— Design a rug. How could you show the texture? What shape is your rug? Is the design abstract or does it depict a scene?

Cut circles out of coloured paper and then cut them in half. Create a pattern using the semi-circles, and perhaps add to the design with details in coloured pencil or pen.

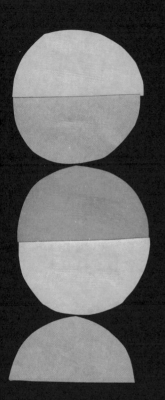

Take some time to continue the pattern below.

Fill the jars with happy memories.

Draw your face three times, very quickly.

Even simple objects can become interesting subjects and inspire creativity. Choose a simple object, such as a piece of fruit. Look at it, then draw it from many different angles. Explore the shape, and how it changes depending on how it is positioned. Use any material, perhaps even cut paper.

Tip: Choose a palette of colours before you start drawing, so that when you begin, you can focus on creating.

Reflect: This activity will encourage you to see the shape of this particular object, rather than just seeing it as 'an apple'. It forces you to consider what you really see, and move away from your expectations of what you think an apple should look like.

Design a mobile.

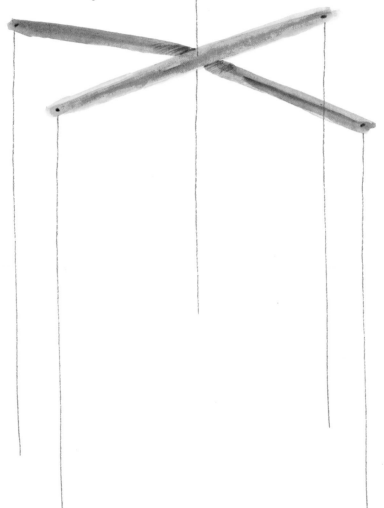

170

Choose 3–5 *analogous* colours from the colour wheel you created in activity 5. Use them to create a piece of art below. You could create an abstract pattern, or perhaps draw a scene in front of you.

Tip: Analogous colours are groups of three or more colours next to each other in your colour wheel. These will form a harmonious palette when used together.

171 —————— Start an 'art pocket' today, where you can store clippings and bits and pieces that inspire you creatively. You could use an envelope, wallet or folder. Whenever you find small items, colours, textures or images that spark ideas, add them to your art pocket. Below, write down some ideas for where you could look.

172 —————— Ask a friend how they bring creativity into their day. Perhaps you can consider ways you can both spend more time being creative. Draw a picture below of your friend being creative in the way they described.

Today, explore using a brush pen, with watercolour paint or ink, to draw something from your home. Remember to consider the shadow of the object too.

Tip: Squint your eyes to better see the areas of light and dark.

Reflect: Consider how the line weights you use help show the weight of an object.

Draw everyday objects from your home using a simple line. Perhaps draw things you see out and about too, or at a friend's home.

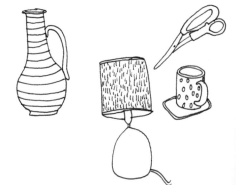

Continue adding to the design.

Design the houses.

177 ——————— Draw warmth.

178 ——————— Design a card for someone you love.

179 ——————— Design some cushions.

180 ——————— Continue the waves then colour in.

Create a series of mini abstract pieces below. Explore mark-making, shape and colour. Allow yourself to be free and loose and try not to overthink it.

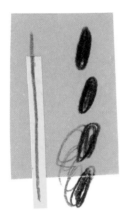

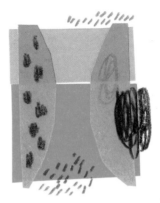

Reflect: Could any of your designs become larger pieces?

Create patterns and designs on the mugs. Perhaps use cut paper, or maybe explore using complementary colours.

183

Fill the page with 'blind' drawings of feet.
This means you should look only at the feet
and shoes while you are drawing,
and not at the page.

You are never out of ideas, it's just that some ideas are more appealing than others. Use the space below to write down as many ideas for creative projects as you can. No matter how small or large, each idea is valid and there is no right or wrong.

Perhaps an idea you are excited by will leap forwards. When you have finished, look through your ideas and circle the ideas you would like to progress now, or at a later date.

Reflect: Look back to where you completed your list earlier on in activity 27. Are there any ideas that you wanted to develop but haven't got around to?

Turn these coloured blobs into vases and jars, and fill them with flowers.

———————— Draw sand, very, very close-up. Capture all the different colours you see.

187 ———————— Design some badges/pins.

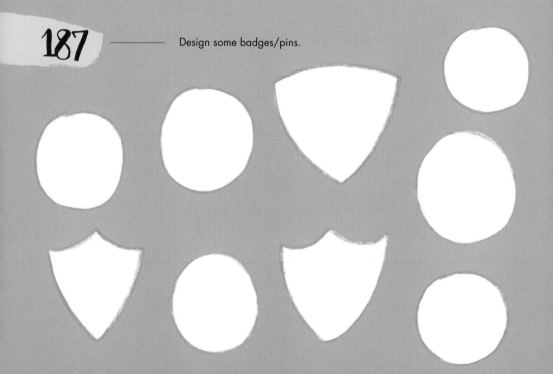

188 ———— Draw a beach.

189 ———— What are your favourite creative exercises so far? How could you develop them further?

190 —————— Draw a night-time scene.

Add colour to the pencils.

192 ——————— Add colour to the pattern. Perhaps where the shapes join you could add the colour that would be created when the two colours either side are mixed.

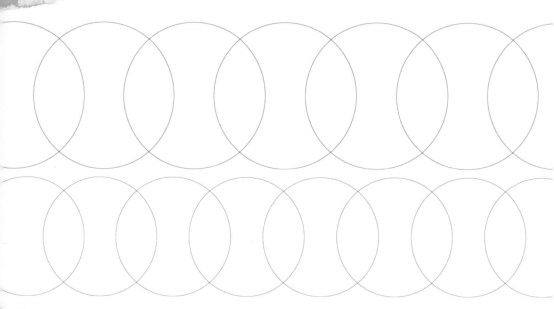

193 ——————— Draw some hats.

194 —————— Fill the space with a pattern that uses geometric shapes.

195 —————— Add designs to the moths' wings.

196

Something we can do when we are searching for creative inspiration is speak to friends or family about ideas. Choose someone you trust, and ask them if they have any ideas about how you could get creative. Write the tips they give here, or launch straight into a piece of art.

Reflect: You don't have to take on board any of the suggestions, but perhaps the ideas put forward will help clarify in your mind what you would like to explore creatively.

197 ——————— Draw a ship on the sea. Or perhaps some fishing boats. You could collage paper to create the shapes of the boats.

199

Draw the sky as quickly as you can. Enjoy freedom and movement with your pen and brush. Really look at the colours and textures.

Tip: You could leave areas of white space within your drawing, to suggest clouds, space and light.

200

Thumbnail sketches can help you quickly see if a composition or colour palette is going to be successful, and if it will inspire a more sustained piece of artwork. Fill the page with small thumbnail drawings of things you can see around you. Use blocks of colour rather than line.

Tip: Try different scales. Some thumbnails could be very zoomed in on an object, and others could be zoomed out, showing a larger scene.

Reflect: Which of your thumbnail sketches could work as larger artworks? What is making the drawing successful?

Don't be scared to make mistakes, embrace them. Make a mistake now – a scribble, or a weird mark – then try to make something out of it.

201

Use these swatches to create a drawing of a face. Only use these colours, and avoid using black. There's no right or wrong way, just enjoy using colours you may not naturally reach for.

202

Writing a creative journal everyday can help you to be more creative generally. Write a few lines below about your day, and what you've enjoyed seeing and learning.

203 —————— Find out when sunset is today, and be ready with your materials 1 hour before. Draw the colours you see in the sky every 10 minutes. Observe how much the colours change over a short period of time.

60 minutes before sunset	*50 minutes before sunset*
40 minutes before sunset	*30 minutes before sunset*
20 minutes before sunset	*10 minutes before sunset*

Use these pages to explore mark-making, and the variety of textures you can create using different materials.

Tip: Try using pencils and oil pastels on their side, to create thicker, rougher marks.

Tip: Experiment with applying varying amounts of pressure to materials as you use them.

Tip: Explore layering.

Reflect: How could you use and explore mark-making in further projects?

205 ———————— Draw different hairstyles.

206 ———————— Create patterns on each of the squares.

207 ——— Fill with a flower pattern.

208 ——— Turn these into characters.

209 ————— Draw some people using a limited colour palette of just 4–8 colours, and avoiding black. Sometimes we reach for black as a habit, without considering if what we are looking at really is true black. Spend around 10 minutes on each drawing.

Design a postcard and write a letter to someone imaginary.

Fill the jars.

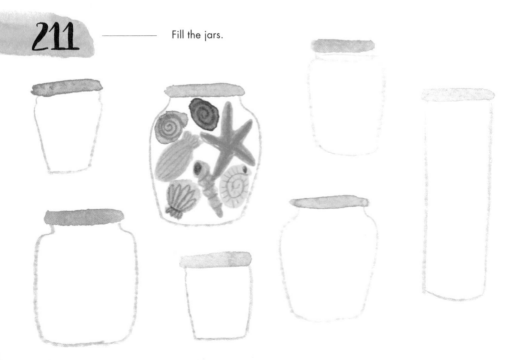

212——— Add designs to the leaves.

213

Spend some time today observing the negative space around objects in your home. Perhaps look at lamps, chairs and plants. Draw only the shapes you see around an object, rather than the object itself.

Reflect: This technique can be used in any drawing to help you understand the space an object takes up and draw more accurately as a result.

Design a mosaic.

216

Pick any exercise you have done so far, and recreate your work below, either using a different style altogether, or just thinking about which areas you would like to change this time around.

217 ——————

Create some quick sketches of people interacting. Try to show movement, and note down any interesting bits of conversation.

Tip: If there is no one nearby to draw, perhaps draw from the television, or online videos.

218 ———— Draw a summer landscape around these trees. Add leaves to the trees and consider summer activities that may be going on.

219 ———— Design some pots or crockery that could be made in clay.

Explore using brush-tip pens and the variety of colours available. Or perhaps continue the pattern using a different material.

221 ———— Continue the pattern.

222 ———— Fill the area with dots. Relax and enjoy choosing colours.

— Add detail to this bunch of flowers. Add stems, leaves and a vase too.

224 ———————— Create an abstract drawing or collage below based on your current mood.

Reflect: Which colours represent your mood? Are there certain marks which help to describe how you feel? Perhaps long sweeping brush marks for a calm mood, and shorter, quicker marks if you feel more unsettled?

225 —————— Mix watercolour paint and water in a palette, dip in your finger or thumb and create watercolour fingerprints on the page. Create abstract shapes, objects or even characters from the marks you make.

226 ———— Design a logo. Perhaps it's for yourself, or an imaginary business, or a business you've always dreamed of having. Sketch out some ideas first, and think about colours.

227 ———— Fill the pots with whatever you like. You could also decorate the pots, add in the surface they are on, and any other objects.

Add faces, hair and shoulders to create people. Draw the eyes about halfway down the head. Consider what distinctive features each face could have. Glasses? Accessories? Hairstyles?

Find a font or piece of lettering that you admire. Replicate it here, and note down where you saw it.

230 ——————— Draw a volcano erupting.

231 ———— Create a scene or graphic design using this background colour and cut-out paper. Perhaps some striking images of birds.

If you are feeling inspired to draw, you can find subject matter all around you. Even observing everyday tasks, such as someone hanging the washing to dry, could be a good opportunity to draw the human figure. Draw a person doing an everyday task.

Tip: Don't worry at all about accuracy here – just enjoy being in the moment, and take the opportunity to study the human form. You may want to work very quickly, so embrace mistakes and keep drawing!

Tip: If your subject is moving a lot, look carefully at their pose and angles of their limbs. Try to fix the image in your mind, before quickly drawing it down on the page.

Practise different marks, textures and materials on each of these fish scales.

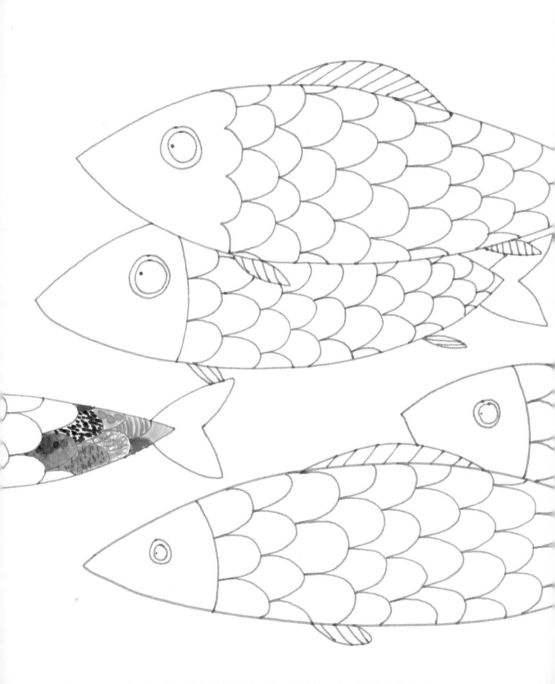

234 ———— Draw an object from your bedroom from memory.

235 ———— What are in the bell jars?

236

Draw an object using only blocks of colour, rather than an outline.

Tip: Try using the edge of an oil pastel or coloured pencil, to create a large surface area.

237

Fill the page with swatches of watercolour. The colours may bleed together, so enjoy the effect when they do. Explore mixing colours in a paint palette before applying them here.

238 ——————— Design a poster for yourself, with a creative mantra or empowering word. Consider the lettering you create, as well as the colours.

Take inspiration from these colour swatches to create a tropical beach. Perhaps there are parrots and other birds. Add in your own swatches of colour, to build the palette.

240 —————— Create a pattern using only curved lines and shapes.

241 —————— Draw plants growing up the trellis.

Create designs on these tiles using cut paper. You could use block shapes, and add detail in pen or coloured pencil.

Tip: Lay pieces of coloured paper alongside each other to see which colours will look striking when used together.

243 ——————— Fill the page with things that fly. Perhaps planes, butterflies, birds and leaves.

———— Decorate the pots and add plants.

Using your non-dominant hand (so if you are right-handed, use your left hand), draw a scene in front of you or a selection of objects. This is tricky so you will need to really focus. You could challenge yourself by using many colours, or just stick to one.

Reflect: This can be a great distraction from busy life, as you will need to use all your concentration.

246 —————— Draw people you love into these frames. Perhaps also design wallpaper behind them.

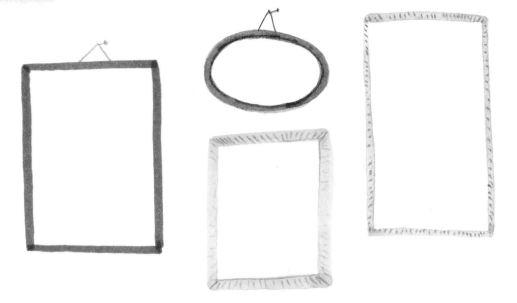

247 —————— Consider how just a few lines can be used to communicate an object. Explore using as few lines and marks as possible to portray a tree.

248 ——————— Be sure to make time for yourself to be creative every day. Write down when you can take a break in your day to add in creativity. What could you do in this time?

249 ——————— Design some cookies or biscuits. What icing would you choose?

250

Design the Russian dolls.

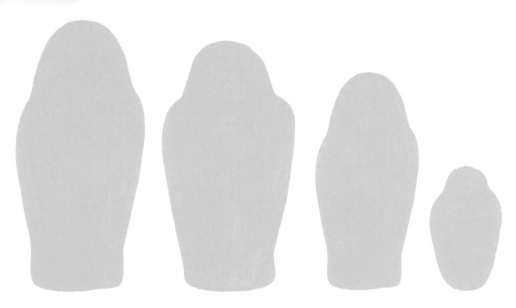

251

Just using torn or cut paper, create a vehicle.

252

Inspiration for your creative projects can come from anywhere. Sit somewhere in your home where you don't frequently sit. Draw six things you haven't noticed before.

Tip: Spend a couple of minutes just looking, before you start. Perhaps you notice the shape of objects or a group of colours you like.

Create designs for pots. Consider the shape, colours and patterns.

Tip: There is plenty of space to experiment here, so don't overthink your designs. Allow yourself to make mistakes and create and explore without any pressure.

254 ———— If you feel like drawing a human figure or face, you always have a subject – yourself! Stand or sit by a mirror, and sketch your face. Perhaps you choose to focus on particular features, like your eyes or nose, or draw the whole face. Don't worry about mistakes, the purpose of this activity is to practise looking, and you can repeat this activity whenever you feel inspired.

Design clothes on the hangers. Consider interesting prints and patterns.

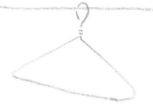

Create a pattern or design in each of the circles. Have fun with it!

257 ———————— Design a bag. What's inside?

258 ———————— Design a chair.

Use the squares and grids to make patterns in each block.

260 ———————— The sky isn't just blue. Fill the page with swatches of all the different colours you have seen in the sky.

261 ———————— Fill the space below with drawings of the sun.

Continue adding branches and leaves to the tree.

263 ——————— Draw a musical instrument. Is it being played? How could you draw music?

264 ——————— Fill this area with red. Orangey-red, pinky-red, different textures and marks.

Reflect: How does red make you feel? What is the mood? How could you use red in your artwork to evoke certain moods?

265 ———————— Draw a person you know, from memory. It could be an abstract drawing, with wild colours and pattern.

266 ———————— Using only these geometric shapes, draw your favourite animal.

267 ———————— Find a photograph that you like. Look at the colours in the image and pick out a colour palette from them. Swatch the colours below.

Reflect: What could you use this palette for?

268 ——————— Draw stripes in different materials.

269

Use this page to complete a series of 'blind' drawings. This means drawing an object without looking at your page, just focusing on looking carefully at the object.

Tip: These drawings aren't about accuracy – your sketches may look a little wild! Instead it's a great way to focus the mind on what you are drawing, and really look at how an object is put together.

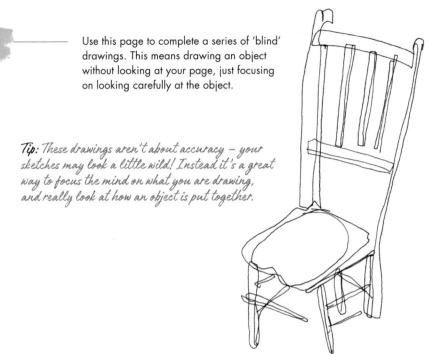

Continue the pattern on the tiles or create your own designs.

Draw all the ingredients for your favourite recipe.

———————— Create rainbows using different materials and colours.

273 ———— Refer back to activity 40 where we completed studies of parts of a scene or human figure, in preparation for a more sustained drawing of a complex scene or posture. Here is the opportunity to use what you've learnt through these drawings to help inform how you approach drawing the whole scene.

Tip: If there is an area of the drawing you feel intimidated by, then take a separate sheet of paper or sketchbook, and explore drawing just this one part, until you feel more comfortable.

Reflect: What did you like about your practice sketches? Perhaps a line quality, or a particular material?

Create islands.

———

Complete a number of 30-second drawings. Choose a subject: perhaps a person, a pet or an object in your home. Using a timer to keep track, draw what you see for 30 seconds, before starting a new drawing. You will need to work quickly, and focus on capturing the key features of your subject.

Tip: You may not want to focus too much on the drawing being accurate, and instead focus on communicating the character and personality of what you are drawing.

Continue the pattern so that it fills the page.

277

Fill each square with a different mark. You could use a variety of materials, and explore the different effects you can get from each one.

278 —————— Drawings don't need to be complicated and busy. Consider how just a few lines and marks can be used to represent an object we are familiar with. Explore using as few lines as possible to show fruit.

279 ———— Colours can be used to express certain moods. How do you feel today? What moods are you experiencing? Show them below using only colour and mark-making.

280 ———— Use a fineliner pen to draw a detailed pattern below.

281 ———————— Complete a 'blind' drawing of yourself: standing by a mirror, draw your reflection without looking at the page. Focus on your face, the distances between your features and the connection between them.

Tip: You may like to use a fineliner pen for this, so that your drawing doesn't smudge as you sketch.

Continue the pattern using different materials.

Visit a café or somewhere out and about. It could be anywhere there are people, or interesting subjects to draw. Draw people and the scenery around them to give them a sense of place.

Tip: Are they eating or drinking? Perhaps there are chairs around them? Or other people?

Tip: Before you go out, create a condensed pencil case of materials. Perhaps just a few colouring pencils, a small watercolour palette, some brush tip pens and fineliners. Try not to take too much with you, as this can be overwhelming when you are sitting in a small space. Anything you feel you've forgotten? Note it down for next time.

Use these black backgrounds to make three dramatic designs. You could explore using bold, graphic shapes in cut-out paper.

Put on some music and create a collage or painting based on what you are listening to. What is the mood? How does it make you feel and how could you express that?

Fill the whole page with different colour watercolour paint strokes. Try different sized strokes, and see how the colours blend.

287 ———————— Draw a peacock's feather. Consider which materials might work well for this.

288 ———————— Design an imaginary underwater animal or fish.

Design a planet from your imagination.

Create a page of planets and stars using oil pastels and watercolour paint. First, draw your planets using the pastels, as these will repel the watercolour when you then paint black over the top. You could also add details to the planets afterwards using coloured pencil.

Create patterns between the lines using just black and white.

Create abstract cross-sections of fruit, real or imaginary. You could use paper collage and then a brush-pen to add details like stalks or seeds.

Tip: When cutting shapes out of the paper you may have to use a bit of trial and error. First, cut a shape larger than you expect to need, see if it fits, then trim if not.

Reflect: Once completed, you could turn your designs into a pattern.

───────

Draw lots of little pictures of all the everyday objects that you have used today.

When drawing out and about, look for interesting views and unusual angles. Visit a café and draw a view that interests you. Perhaps through a doorway, window, or in the corner of the room. Perhaps someone is partially hidden, and you just see parts of them through an object.

Tip: You don't have to draw everything in the scene, as this can feel overwhelming. Instead, focus on the key elements and points of interest.

Tip: Perhaps start with a quick sketch of the scene, before adding colour, so you can map out the positions of everything in relation to each other.

Design the cakes. You may also want to add patterns and colour to the cake cases.

——————— Fill with rain drops.

We are surrounded by potential sources of inspiration, even when carrying out ordinary tasks in our day-to-day lives. The simplest object, such as a sliced vegetable or piece of fruit, could become the subject of your art.

1. Start by choosing an everyday object as your subject and observe it for a while. Perhaps certain colour combinations catch your eye. You could start by drawing the 'negative space' around the object. For example, the plate around these tomatoes.

2. Build up the colours in blocks. You could use a variety of materials – whatever feels right to you in that moment. What are the key shapes that you notice? Are there any areas of brightness or white?

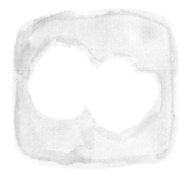

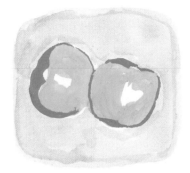

3. Add details. Notice the variety of colours and shapes. Focus on drawing what you see, rather than what you expect to see. We often have preconceptions about what everyday items look like . . . what does it truly look like?

4. Add highlights and shadow. You may want to add some additional context around the drawing. Maybe a table surface, some objects in the background. Or perhaps you leave the focus on the object itself.

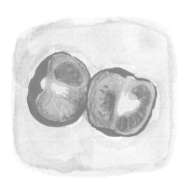

298 ——————— Create a pattern using oil pastel and watercolour. Draw with the oil pastel first, and then add watercolour on top. The oil based pastels will repel the watercolour, and so the bright colours will show through.

Draw your home from memory. Perhaps fill the page with drawings of things you enjoy in your home too – it could be quite abstract.

300 ———— Continue adding to the design.

You are never out of
ideas; some might just
be better than others.
Write down or sketch
all the ideas you have
for a creative project,
whether you think they
are successful or not.

301

Draw the shapes and lines you see when you close your eyes.

——————— What is on the shelf? Ornaments? Plants? Your favourite books?

303 ——————— Use the space below to design a painted frame for a print, photograph or piece of artwork. If you create a design you like, you could paint a real frame and hang it in your home.

Draw people very quickly, using a black fineliner pen. Go somewhere busy to make your drawings, like a café, restaurant or somewhere in a town.

305

Draw a horizon that you can see, but start by drawing the negative space of the sky. Then add in what you see beneath the sky.

Continue the design using cut paper. You could also use patterns that you find in magazines.

307

Draw an autumn landscape around these trees. Add autumnal foliage and perhaps some wildlife.

308

Draw flowers from your imagination. Invent your own varieties.

309 ——————— Using the skills you practised in activity 80, create repeat patterns using the mono-print technique.

Tip: As you will be using oil pastels this can get a bit messy. Once you've completed your drawing, you may like to protect your page from smudging by attaching a layer of tracing paper, or by spraying with a fixative.

310

Draw the same object using four different materials. Perhaps try collage, a pencil drawing, paint and mixed media. Perhaps try drawing it first in colour, and then in black and white.

Reflect: Which material do you enjoy using the most?

Material:

Material:

Material:

Material:

Fill a page with lots of pencil sketches of people. Perhaps visit a café, library, or even draw on a train journey.

Tip: If your subject moves, you could draw their new position right on top of the old drawing. Here, the lady moved her hand position, and I drew it twice. It helps to tell a story about what was happening.

Reflect: Working in pencil means you can draw quickly, and also not worry too much about mistakes.

312 ———— Draw your legs and feet when they are stretched out in front of you. Are there any shadows? How could you show the texture of your clothes?

Create designs on the eggs. Are they real eggs? Or decorative?

314 ——————— Consider how just a few lines can be used to represent a person. Explore using as few lines and marks as possible to portray a figure.

315 ——————— Write some short notes to yourself. What advice for creativity would you like to remember?

316

Using only these colours below, plus black and white, create an abstract image of some household objects, such as bowls, books or bottles. Using a limited palette will encourage you to concentrate on the shapes of the objects, and there is no need to worry about the colours not being a true representation of what you see.

317

Fill the bowl with fruit. You could add other things on to the table around the bowl too – like other foods or bowls.

318 ——————— Design some toys.

Turn these into faces, characters and masks. Could it be a carnival?

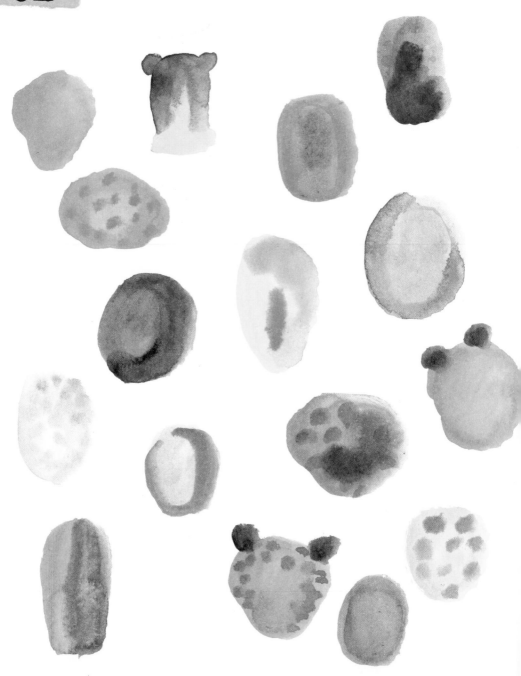

320 ——————— Fill the page with pineapple or other tropical fruits. Perhaps you could make a repeat pattern, or explore using different materials in a variety of ways to create all your fruit.

Try a partially 'blind' drawing, where you only occasionally look at the page to get your bearings. Choose a subject that inspires you, and keep looking at it as you draw. Spend the majority of the time looking carefully at the colours and shapes in front of you, rather than the paper, even as you add colour to the page.

Tip: Use a variety of materials and pick up whatever feels right in the moment. You may want to prepare by having a lot of materials around you before you start.

Reflect: By not worrying too much about accuracy and whether you are drawing things in the right place, you can focus on the energy of the drawing, and create very loose, exciting pieces of art.

322

You are never out of ideas, it's just that some ideas are more appealing than others. Use the space below to write down as many ideas for creative projects as you can. No matter how small or large, each idea is valid and there is no right or wrong.

Perhaps an idea you are excited by will leap forwards. When you have finished, look through your ideas and circle the ideas you would like to progress now, or at a later date.

Reflect: Look back to your completed lists earlier on in activities 27 and 184. Are there any ideas that you wanted to develop but haven't got around to?

323 ———— Draw the creature that has made these prints.

324 ———— Design three clocks.

325 ———— Fill the page with images of fish and coral. Consider the patterns on their fins and bodies. Perhaps use cut paper and bold shapes, adding finer detail in coloured pencil.

326 ——————— Use a brush pen and watercolour, or another material that allows you to work quickly, such as oil pastel. Explore drawing figures using simple shapes and lines.

327 —————— To help inspire creativity every day, you could keep a creative journal. Try this out by writing an entry here. Note down ideas, and any creative thoughts you have today. If your mind is blank, start by just writing down a few key words from your day.

328 —————— Draw a rainbow.

329

Add lampshades to the lights. Consider unusual designs, patterns and prints. Perhaps use cut paper to create bold shapes.

330 —— Add smiley faces.

Fill the jar with all the ingredients you'd need for a positive day.

332 ——

When you make a drawing, it can be interesting to work into some parts of it more than others. For example, you could spend most of the time on the face, and then represent the clothing with simple lines and colour. This can help add character and energy to your artwork. Try this technique below.

333

Fill the page with fruit and vegetables, so that they are all touching.

Decorate the tins.

Design balloons.

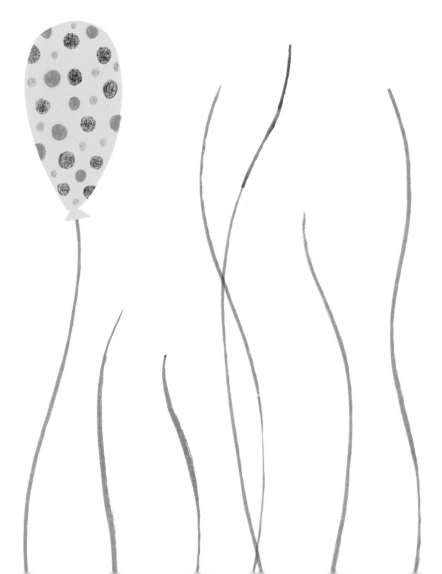

336 —————— It is very important to keep positive about your creative output. Even if the end result isn't what you expected, remember how you enjoyed the time spent being creative. Write some positive reminders to yourself now about your creative work.

Reflect: What are you good at? How have you improved?

337 —————— Draw a bang!

338 ——————— Fill the page with multi-coloured tear-drop shapes. Use a variety of materials.

339 ———— Design some fossils.

340 ——————— Draw your bedroom.

Design a poster about love.

342

Create swatches of autumnal colours.

343

Draw the cold.

344

Fill the squares with concentric circles.

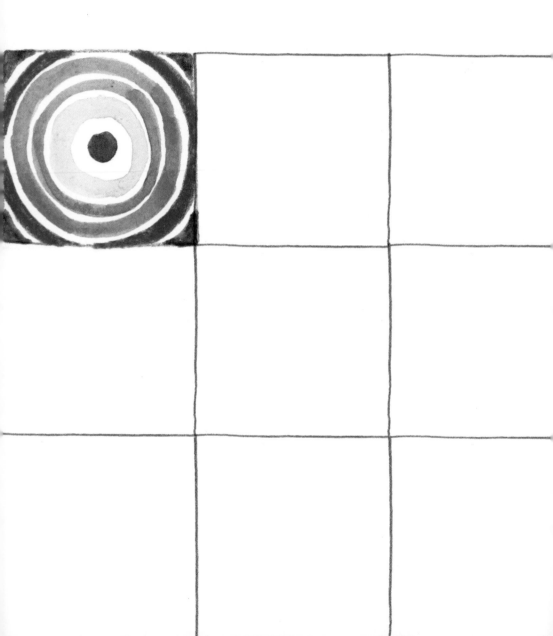

345 ———— Create a pattern using triangles.

346 ———— Fill the space with tulip flowers, using different combinations of materials.

347 ———— Design some playing cards. What would the Queen look like?
Or the Joker?

You could collect pebbles and paint designs onto them using acrylics. Draw designs onto the stones here, to explore your ideas.

349　————

Draw animals but rather than drawing them in the correct colours, use the colours and prints of different animals. A leopard-print crocodile? A leathery-grey flamingo? A pink-feathered elephant?

350 ——————— Open up a drawer in your house and draw what you find inside.

351

There are lots of ways you can overcome the fear associated with a blank space, and the worry about how to start. Today, begin with a graphic shape and see where your mind takes you.

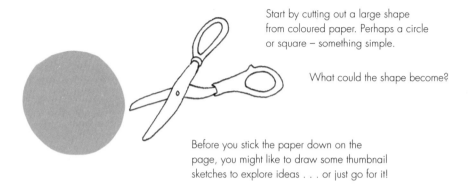

Start by cutting out a large shape from coloured paper. Perhaps a circle or square – something simple.

What could the shape become?

Before you stick the paper down on the page, you might like to draw some thumbnail sketches to explore ideas . . . or just go for it!

    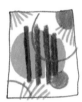

Perhaps you will want to cut into the shape more, or maybe the whole thing becomes a background or part of a scene.

Sketch some thumbnail ideas here:

Paste your shapes here:

Who do these feet belong to? Try using a variety of materials.

353

Add life into the terrariums.

354 ——————— Draw a planet. Is it a planet with lots of water? Desert? Does it have rings? Or moons?

355

Fill the page with bamboo.
Practise controlling the thickness
of the brush and applying different
amounts of pressure to create
a varying thickness of line.

356 ——— Writing down your thoughts can help unclog a creative block, as it gets your mind thinking freely. Write some lines about your day, and any ideas you have about creativity.

357 ——— Fill the space with leaves. Consider colours other than green.

Colour in the polka dots.

359

Imagine the centre of this page is a mirror. Draw the reflection of this abstract drawing on the opposite page. Try to make your colours as similar as possible.

360

Think about where you would most like to be right now. Imagine the doorway below has a view to that place and draw what you might see.

361

Design prints and patterns on the socks.
You could even use cut paper.

362 —— Fill these pages with collages of everyday objects. Perhaps lots of vases of flowers, from imagination or studies from life. Use a variety of materials.

Tip: Try layering tissue paper over coloured paper for an interesting effect.

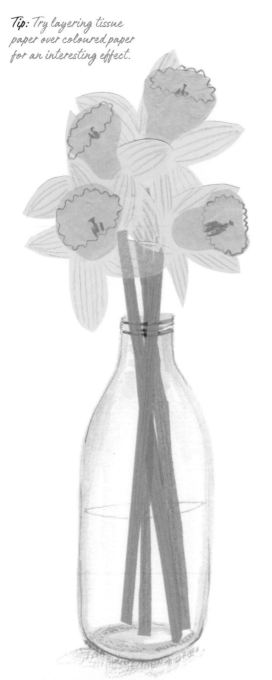

363 ——————— Draw today's clouds. Consider all the different colours you can see, and how you could show movement and weather with expressive marks.

Fill the page with circles in any material you like.

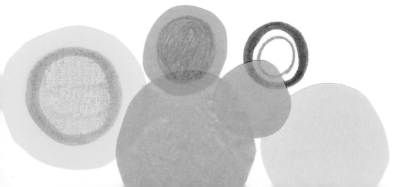

365

Add colourful patterns to the shapes using a set of three analogous colours for each design.

Bring creativity
into your everyday life.
Seek it out. Be inspired
by shape, colour and
pattern wherever you go.
How can you make your
day more creative?

Goal review

Look back at your creative goals at the beginning of the year. You may like to write a few lines on the opposite page about your experiences, perhaps noting down anything you've learnt, tips for yourself or artistic projects you'd like to continue. Be positive and encouraging.

Reflect on these questions:

Did you achieve your goals?

What have you improved at during the process of completing the 365 activities?

What areas would you like to continue to develop?

Which tasks do you enjoy doing? Could you continue exploring these in your own sketchbook?

Are there any materials you particularly enjoyed using? Or materials that you'd like to explore further?

It's absolutely fine if you didn't achieve your goals as your interests and how you would like to progress your creative journey will naturally change as you spend more time being creative.

The only thing that really matters is that you feel positive about creating, and enjoy it!

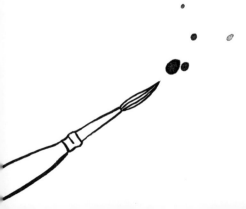

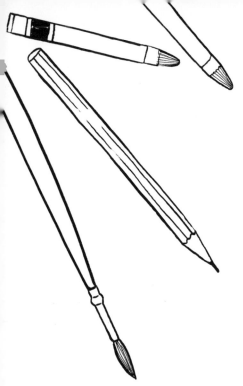

About the Author

Lorna Scobie grew up in the depths of the English countryside, climbing trees and taking her rabbit for walks in the fields. She is an illustrator and designer, now based in south London. Growing up surrounded by nature has heavily influenced her illustrations and her work often revolves around the natural world and animal kingdom.

Lorna draws every day, and always has a sketchbook close to hand when she's out and about, just in case. She illustrates her work by hand rather than digitally, as she enjoys the spontaneity and also the 'happy mistakes' that can happen along the way. Her favourite places to draw are museums and botanical gardens.

This is the third book in Lorna's 365 Days series, following on from *365 Days of Art* and *365 Days of Drawing*.

If you'd like to keep up to date with Lorna's work, she can be found on Instagram and Twitter: **@lornascobie**

www.lornascobie.com